FAMILY
CELEBRATIONS

FAMILY CELEBRATIONS

by
Diane Patrick

ILLUSTRATED BY
Michael Bryant

SILVER MOON PRESS
NEW YORK

For information contact
Silver Moon Press
126 Fifth Avenue, Suite 803,
New York, New York 10011
First Edition

Distributed to the trade by
August House
PO Box 3223
Little Rock, Arkansas 72203
(800) 284-8784

Designed by Tilman Reitzle

Cover Illustration by Michael Bryant

Printed in the United States of America

Library of Congress
Cataloging-in-Publication Data

ISBN: 1-881889-04-1

The Publisher would like to extend its gratitude
to the Family Counseling Services,
Westhampton Beach, New York,
for its cooperation and assistance in reviewing this book.

TABLE OF CONTENTS

CHAPTER ONE

You're Invited!

ॐ

WHEN SOMETHING GOOD happens to you, who shares your joy?

If something bad happens, to whom do you tell your troubles? Your family, that's who.

Right now, you are probably close to your family—whether you like it or not! If you live with your family, they share every day of your life.

Of course, you might not live with all of your family members. So when the whole family is together, it can be a real celebration.

Most families gather for special events like births, weddings, and funerals. These things occur all over the world. We all celebrate the birth of a child, or the marriage of two people in love. And all people want to share their sadness when someone they love dies.

Other family times may not be such big deals, but they are fun anyway. When does your family get together? At Thanksgiving? On the Fourth of July? Even going to the park can be a special family event.

This book will tell you how different kinds of families share extra-special times.

ช

CHAPTER TWO

The Beginning of Life

ॐ

THE BIRTH OF A CHILD is a special time for families.

Proud parents let the world know when they have a baby.

They send letters to friends and relatives. They put notices in newspapers. Happy friends and relatives will visit the newest family member.

Many families have a ceremony for a new-born baby. The ceremony will name the child. Or it will welcome the child to the world. Some will introduce the baby to the family religion.

Different religions have different ceremonies for babies. Christians have a baptism, or a christening. Jewish boys have a *bris* when they are only eight days old. In

Islam, there is a similar ceremony for boys
called a *tahara*. Hindu babies are named in
the *namakaran* ceremony.

How does your family celebrate the
arrival of a new child? Does the ceremony
have a special name?

This story is about a christening.

*The entire family loves a baby. This grandmother holds
her grandson at a family reunion.*

"The Truth About Babies"

ঌ

BABIES STINK, LUCY THOUGHT. She was watching TV. A commercial came on. It showed happy parents playing with a tiny baby.

They always show cute, happy babies on TV, Lucy thought. But they don't show you the truth about babies. For instance, they don't show you how babies cry all night long. Or how babies make big messes in their diapers. Or how that makes them stink!

Just then the phone rang. Lucy got up and answered it.

"Hello—who is this?" asked a frantic voice.

"This is Lucy."

"Lucy, this is Aunt Joan. Is your mother or father at home?"

"No," Lucy said. "They took the baby next door."

"Oh, dear," Aunt Joan said. "Lucy, could you give your mother a very important message?"

"Of course," Lucy said.

"Tell your mother that our car has broken down," Aunt Joan said. "We'll be late for the baptism. Tell her we'll get there as soon as we can. But I don't know how soon that will be."

"Don't worry, I'll tell her," Lucy said. She hung up the phone and went back to the sofa to watch TV.

The commercials were over by then. The baseball game was back on. Lucy settled in to watch.

Lucy knew in the back of her mind that she should turn off the TV. Her parents had told Lucy to change into her new dress while they were next door. But the game was just getting good. So Lucy decided to watch one more inning. Besides, there was lots of time before she had to go to the church.

"Lucy!" snapped a voice.

Lucy looked up. Her mom and dad stood by the door. Behind them stood Grandma. Lucy's mom held Lucy's baby sister, Grace.

"Why haven't you changed your clothes?" Lucy's mom asked.

"The game is on," Lucy explained. "The score is tied up."

"That's no excuse, young lady," Lucy's mom said. "I told you to change. We can't be late for the baptism!"

That reminded Lucy of Aunt Joan's message. "Mom, I've got something to tell you," Lucy said.

"There's no time," her mom said, as she rushed through the living room.

"But—" Lucy began.

"No buts!" her dad told Lucy sternly. "Please go to your room and change into your dress. Now!"

"Yes, sir," Lucy said. She pouted and walked to her room. "I'll help," Lucy's grandma said. She followed Lucy into her room.

Lucy was angry. In her bedroom, she pulled on her frilly white dress. "Grandma, why do we have to go to church?" Lucy asked. "It's not even Sunday."

"Don't you want to welcome your baby sister into the world?"

"I don't have to," Lucy said. "She's already here. Besides, Mom and Dad spend all of their time with her. She doesn't need me to welcome her."

Her grandma looked at Lucy.

"The truth is, your sister is a helpless baby," she said. "So of course your parents spend a lot of time looking after her. Today, Aunt Joan and Uncle Eric will promise to look after Grace, too. That's why we are all meeting in church today. To show that we all care about baby Grace—and each other."

Soon, Lucy was at the church with her parents and Grandma. A group of her aunts, uncles, and cousins was there, too.

The priest came down the aisle and greeted Lucy's parents. He tickled Grace's chin, saying "cootchy-coo." Her cries filled the church. The priest smiled.

"If everyone is here, why don't we begin?" he said.

"I'm afraid we're not all here," Lucy's mom said. She was upset. "The godmother—my sister Joan—is late. But I'm sure she'll be here soon. I don't know what could be keeping her."

Aunt Joan! Lucy thought. She had forgotten all about the message! Lucy stepped forward and tugged on her mother's skirt.

"What is it?" her mother asked Lucy.

Lucy told her. Then Lucy shut her eyes and looked away. She expected her parents to be mad at her for forgetting the message.

"It's all right," Lucy's father said. "Lucy tried to tell us about their delay, but I wouldn't listen."

The priest looked at his watch. "We could wait, I suppose," he said. "But there is a baseball game on TV, and I'd like to see the end of it. Why doesn't someone stand in for the godmother?"

"You mean, someone could take Joan's place?" Lucy's mom asked.

"Yes," the priest said. "It would just be for the ceremony."

Lucy's parents and grandmother gathered together. They talked to each other in low voices. Then they turned to Lucy.

"Lucy, would you like to stand in for Aunt Joan?" Lucy's father asked.

"Your sister needs you," her mother added.

Lucy felt proud during the ceremony. She held Grace in her arms, while the priest asked some questions. Lucy and her Uncle Eric—the godfather—answered for the baby. At the end of the ceremony, the priest sprinkled water on Grace's forehead. She began to cry.

"Shhhh," Lucy said. She rocked Grace in her arms. Grace stopped crying. Her eyes darted across Lucy's face. Then the corners of her tiny mouth turned up.

She smiled at me! Lucy thought.

Just then, there was a commotion at the back of the church. Aunt Joan and Uncle Mike rushed in.

"Are we too late?" Aunt Joan asked.

"No," Lucy said. She looked at her parents and grandma. They were smiling at Lucy, too.

"The truth is, we are all here to look after baby Grace," Lucy explained.

੩ၑ

CHAPTER THREE

Coming of Age

ᨠ

WHEN ARE YOU NO LONGER A CHILD?
That depends. As you grow up, things change. Your body changes. Your way of thinking changes. And the way you get along with your family changes, too.

Many families celebrate when a boy or girl is no longer a child. You could call this a coming-of-age celebration. Jewish boys and girls have bar mitzvahs and bat mitzvahs. Catholic boys and girls have first Communions. Catholic teens have confirmation.

Not all coming-of-age parties are religious. Many girls have a "Sweet Sixteen" party on their sixteenth birthday. Some families have a party when a son or daughter graduates from school.

What celebration are you looking forward to? How old will you be when it takes place?

This story describes a boy's bar mitzvah.

This Irish girl is going to have her first Communion—a Catholic "coming of age" ceremony.

Zak and the
Battling Aunts

ව

"**D**IE, ALIEN, DIE!"
Zak laughed at his friend John.

The two boys were playing a video game in John's basement. A crowd of kids had gathered around them. They saw John blast Zak's spaceship and win the game.

"Nice shooting, John!" someone called out.

"I only let him win because it's his birthday," Zak said.

"Then how did I manage to beat you five times yesterday?" John asked. Everyone laughed, including Zak.

Zak was at John's thirteenth birthday party. The party was in the basement of John's house. There was food, music, and games. The only people there were John and his friends.

A few hours later the party ended. As Zak walked up the stairs, John patted him on the back. "Thanks for the new game cartridge," John said.

"That's what best friends are for," Zak said with a grin.

"What time should I show up for your birthday party next week?" John asked.

The smile left Zak's face. "Oh, whenever," he said. He looked out the back door. His mother was waiting in a car in the driveway. "I've got to go. Bye!" Zak rushed out the door and into the car.

"How was the party?" Zak's mother asked as they rode home.

"Great," Zak said.

Especially compared to what his party would be like, Zak thought. Thinking of his birthday party put Zak in a bad mood. Zak wished he could have a party like John's. Instead, he was going to have a bar mitzvah.

Zak's bar mitzvah would take place at a temple, or synagogue. Afterward, all of Zak's family and friends would gather for a party at his house.

Zak had to study for the bar mitzvah ceremony. There, he would give blessings and read from the Torah, or the holy book. It was written in a foreign language, called Hebrew. Zak had to work hard to learn how to read it.

The studying did not bother Zak. He and his friends in Hebrew school had fun studying together.

Zak did not like the fact that he had to invite his whole family to the party. That included his two old aunts, Esther and Sarah. They loved to bicker and argue! Zak was sure his aunts would embarrass him in front of his friends.

"Why do I have to invite everyone in the family?" Zak had asked his father. "Why can't I just invite my friends?"

Zak's father smiled. "The more the merrier!" was all he said.

At last came the day of Zak's bar mitzvah.

Zak stood in the synagogue and read from the Torah. He looked out over the people. He saw his parents looking at him proudly. He saw his cousins smiling. He saw his Aunts Esther and Sarah.

Uh-oh, Zak thought. They looked grouchy.

Afterward, everyone went to Zak's house to celebrate.

"Cool party," John said to Zak. The two boys sat together for dinner. "I never knew that you had so many relatives."

"Neither did I," Zak said. "My hand is numb from shaking hands with aunts, uncles, and cousins!" Just then, Zak heard two familiar voices. He groaned. Aunt Esther and Aunt Sarah walked up to the table.

"Do you mind if we join you?" Aunt Esther said as she sat down.

Yes! Zak thought to himself.

"No," John said.

"You must be one of Zak's friends," Aunt Sarah said. She looked at Zak and sighed. "He is such a handsome boy," she declared.

"What boy?" Aunt Esther replied. "Our Zak is a young man!"

Zak flinched. This was it! His aunts were about to get into an argument over whether he was a boy or a young man.

"Esther, you are so right," Aunt Sarah said. She held up her glass. "To the handsome young man!" she said. Aunt Esther joined her, clinking her glass with Sarah's.

After all the guests were gone, John and Zak watched TV together. "Your two aunts are pretty funny," John said.

"Funny?" Zak said, surprised.

"Yes," John said. "I like to hear them tease each other. And their stories are funny. Especially the ones about your dad when he was a kid." John sighed. "My family never sits around talking like that. I wish I had aunts like yours."

The next day, Zak's mom made him write thank-you notes to people who had given him gifts. But he didn't just thank Aunt Esther and Aunt Sarah for the socks they had given him.

"Dear Aunt Esther and Aunt Sarah," Zak wrote. "Thank you for telling all of those great stories."

Zak also wrote, "It's nice to know that your family can also be your friends."

૨☙

On their wedding day, couples promise to love and honor each other for the rest of their lives. This couple wears European-style clothes at their traditional Korean ceremony.

CHAPTER FOUR

Marriages

᷼

MARRIAGE IS AN IMPORTANT family event. Not only do the bride and groom get married, but their families become related.

Some weddings are very large. All of the couple's friends and relatives are invited. At a large wedding, some of the relatives may come from far away. It takes a lot of planning and hard work to have a big wedding.

Other weddings are small. Some people want to celebrate their marriage just with those people they know best. Only the couple's closest friends and relatives will attend.

Big or small, weddings are happy events. After the ceremony, the bride's and groom's families and friends usually go to a party. This party is called a wedding reception. There they all eat, dance, and wish the couple a happy life.

And of course, wedding guests get to

meet new relatives! When people get married, their families are said to be related by marriage. A person who is married may have a new mother-in-law, father-in-law, and brothers- and sisters-in-law.

This story describes a wedding.

The Lonely Groom

੩

"MARIA, YOU ARE SO BEAUTIFUL!" Maria's mother wiped away a tear and blew her nose. Maria stood next to her. Maria was wearing a white wedding dress.

"Oh, please, Mama," Maria said, rolling her eyes. "I'm only trying the dress on. The wedding isn't for another three months!"

Maria and her mother were at the dress store. Maria was picking out a wedding dress. Just three weeks earlier, she had become engaged to her boyfriend, Antonio.

Just then, another young woman came into the room. It was Maria's little sister, Yolanda. She had on a pretty yellow dress.

"How do I look?" Yolanda asked.

Her mother gasped. "Yolanda? Is that you?" she asked in surprise. "My little girl is now a beautiful woman!" she said. Then she began to cry some more.

"Mama is the only woman who would cry at a dress fitting," Maria said with a smile.

"You would think she is used to it by now," Yolanda told Maria. "After all, you're the third daughter to get married!"

Yolanda was happy that her sister was getting married. It meant Yolanda at last would have her own room! She was also happy because her sister and Antonio were very much in love. And besides, Yolanda was going to be the maid of honor.

As maid of honor, Yolanda helped plan the wedding. It was going to be huge. Yolanda's family was very, very big. One day she and Maria went over the guest list. They were checking to see who was coming and who was not.

"Uncle Luis and Aunt Sonia," Maria read from the list.

"They are coming," Yolanda said, reading from hers.

"Cousin Tito and his family."

"They can't make it," Yolanda said.

"Too bad," said Maria. "I haven't seen Tito for years. Well, that's everyone from our side. What is the total?"

Yolanda added up the names. "One hundred and seventy-five people are coming," she said. "And that's just our family!"

"Whew!" Maria said. "That will be a lot of people! Now let's look at Antonio's guest list."

Yolanda took a second list from Maria.

"There must be a mistake," Yolanda said. "This is just the last page. Where are the other pages?"

"There are no other pages. That's everyone Antonio has invited."

Yolanda looked at the list. She was surprised. There were only fifteen names on it. And none of them had Antonio's last name.

Yolanda and Maria quickly went through the list. All of the people had responded. They would all be at the wedding.

"That means we will have almost two hundred guests," Maria said. "What a lot of work it will be!"

But Yolanda was not thinking about the wedding, nor the work it would take. She was wondering why Antonio had not invited any brothers, sisters, aunts, or uncles.

"Does Antonio like to fight and argue?" Yolanda wondered aloud.

"Of course not!" Maria said. "What makes you ask such a thing?"

Yolanda looked at Antonio's short guest list. Why else would he not invite his family—unless he fought with them?

"I was just wondering," Yolanda asked.

"Yolanda, I don't have time for your silly questions," Maria said. "I have to go visit the baker and order the cake. If Antonio comes, tell him where to find me."

As the wedding day drew near, the family grew more excited—and busy! Yolanda looked forward to the day. But she also looked at Antonio closely whenever she saw him.

Antonio was as nice as ever—he was polite and respectful to Maria's family. So why was *his* family not coming to the wedding?

Finally, the wedding day arrived. At the wedding, Yolanda's family completely filled up the left side of the church. There were only a few people on Antonio's side.

Yolanda looked at the people who were there for Antonio. She began to feel sorry for Antonio. Yolanda thought that he must be lonely with no family at his wedding.

Yolanda thought the ceremony was beautiful. The priest blessed Antonio and Maria. He told everyone that they were now husband and wife before God. Antonio and Maria promised to love each other for their whole lives.

After the wedding, Yolanda heard Antonio point out all of his guests to Maria. For each one, he said things like, "He's like an uncle to me," or, "She's like a sister to me."

During the reception, Yolanda saw that the friends seemed to love Antonio. They all hugged and kissed him and smiled proudly.

At the reception, Yolanda sat at the table, thinking things over. The party had been going on for hours. Her aunts were dancing a traditional dance from Mexico. They were laughing, butting heads, and pushing each other. Someone tapped her on the shoulder. It was Antonio.

"Would you care to dance with me?" he asked. Yolanda nodded and followed him to the dance floor.

"You seem very serious today, Yolie," Antonio said. "Aren't you happy for Maria and me?"

"Of course," Yolanda said. "I was just thinking—." She could no longer contain her curiosity. "Antonio—why didn't you invite any of your family to the wedding? Do you fight with them?"

Antonio laughed. "So that's it," he said. "I thought you had been acting strangely. The fact is, Yolie, I don't have any family."

Antonio went on to tell her that he had been an only child. Both his parents had died several years ago.

"I have cousins, but they live in Mexico," Antonio explained. "They are very happy for me, I know."

"I'm sorry about your parents," Yolanda said. "You must be very lonely."

"I miss them," Antonio said. "But I'm not lonely. I have all my friends to share this special day. They share my good times. They comfort me in bad times. They are always there when I need them. And isn't that what a family is all about?"

Yolanda didn't answer Antonio in words. But she gave her new brother-in-law a big hug.

"But now, Yolie, I have a very big family, don't I?" he said.

Yolanda couldn't argue with that!

৵

Different families have different kinds of reunions. The family above went to the beach. The family to the right threw a party in the park.

CHAPTER FIVE

Family Reunions

ॐ

Families have many reasons to come together for a celebration. They often will gather on holidays, birthdays, wedding anniversaries, and other special days.

At times, families will gather for no reason—except to see each other!

For instance, many families have regular family reunions. At these reunions, family members from all over come to one place. They celebrate their ties to each other. The reunions give family members a chance to learn about each other—and themselves.

This story is about a family reunion.

The
Old Lady Name

ॐ

"**E**THEL'S AN OLD LADY NAME! Ethel's an old lady name!"

Ethel's ears burned. She walked quickly through the playground. She ignored the kids as they chanted at her.

For as long as Ethel could remember, kids had made fun of her name. Today, Aisha and Tiffany were teasing her.

"Ethel's an old lady name!" they chanted.

Ethel walked home. It was the first day of summer vacation. Ethel was glad it was summer. At least the teasing stopped then.

Ethel had another reason to be glad it was summer. She and her mom were going to a family reunion. The Davises—her mom's family—was very big. Every three years, they came from all over the country to be together.

One day before the reunion, Ethel's mom showed her a photograph. In it was a lady wearing a military uniform.

"That is your cousin Ethel," Ethel's mom said. "She hasn't been to a reunion in years. But you will meet her at this one."

Ethel looked at the picture. "She's beautiful," Ethel said. "How did she get stuck with this old lady name?"

Ethel's mom laughed. "You were both named after your Great Aunt Ethel. She's no longer with us, but you both keep her name alive."

Ethel was eager to meet her pretty cousin who shared her ugly name.

The day of the reunion arrived. Ethel and her mom drove to Baltimore, where it was being held. When they got to the hotel, Ethel saw a big sign out front. It read, "WELCOME DAVIS FAMILY!" Seeing her family name made Ethel proud.

That night, there was a party for the whole family. As members of the Davis family came in, they each received a shopping bag. It had the following things in it:
   * a list of events that would take place during the weekend,
   * a T-shirt reading "Davis Family Reunion,"
   * a book of family recipes,
   * a family history with photographs and guessing games,
   * two picture frames, and
   * a map of Baltimore that showed places that were special to the Davis family.
At the party, Ethel saw her cousin Ethel. She went up to the pretty woman.

"Hi," Ethel said. "I'm your cousin Ethel."

"Goodness, I remember you when you were tiny," cousin Ethel told her namesake.

"I don't remember you at all," Ethel said. "I was just a baby when we met."

"Well, then, we have some catching up to do," cousin Ethel said. "Let's talk."

The two Ethels sat down.

"Can I ask you a personal question?" little Ethel asked.

"Sure."

"When you were in school, did the other kids tease you about your name?"

Cousin Ethel laughed. "Yes!" she said. "They called me 'Ethylene.' That's a type of fuel. They asked how I got out of the gas tank."

"Hey, that's a good one!" Ethel said.

"I didn't think so," cousin Ethel said. "The teasing used to bother me."

"It did?"

"Yes. But I got over it," cousin Ethel said. "Later, I got to be friends with many of the kids who teased me. In fact, your mother was one of the worst teasers."

"You're kidding!" little Ethel said.

"I don't blame them," cousin Ethel said. "What you are called doesn't mean anything, anyway. It's who you are that counts."

"But why do I have to be called 'Ethel?'"

"We both are named after Aunt Ethel," cousin Ethel said. "She was a great lady. Did you know Aunt Ethel taught high school science?"

"No," little Ethel said.

"She did," her cousin said. "She was the first woman teacher in the family. Aunt Ethel

got me interested in science. I figured if I had her name, I might have her brains, too."

Cousin Ethel then left her young cousin to go visit with others. But she left Ethel a lot to think about.

That night there was a family banquet. Old Uncle Chester, cousin Ethel's dad, stood up.

"I'd like to make an announcement."Uncle Chester smiled proudly. "I am a happy papa today," he said. "Just last week my daughter Ethel finished her training program. My little girl is going to be an Air Force pilot! She's the first pilot in our family!"

Everyone in the family applauded. Young Ethel clapped hardest of all.

When Ethel returned to school, she didn't care as much when kids teased her. She was proud to be Ethel Davis. Ethel worked harder on her math and science. She knew that her family once had a science teacher. Now they had a pilot.

Ethel decided that the Davis family also would have an astronaut, and that she would be it!

❧

Funerals are sad. In this picture, the family of President John Kennedy mourns at his funeral.

CHAPTER SIX

Funerals

&

DEATH IS VERY SAD. But as sad as it is, death is still a part of life.

When a person's life ends, his or her family are the people who are the saddest. Often, they come together to share their grief. Many people have a religious ceremony for a dead person. These are called funerals.

In some cultures, a funeral is not only a time for sadness. It is also a time to remember the life of the person who died. So a funeral not only mourns death, it also celebrates life.

This story describes a Buddhist funeral.

Memories of Grandfather

❧

IT WAS OVER. Ken's grandfather had died the week before. Ken had spent many, many sad hours in the days since.

Grandfather's body had been burned, or cremated. The ashes were put in a simple jar, called an urn. This was taken to the Buddhist temple where Ken and his family worshipped. There, Grandfather's friends and relatives could come to pay their respects to him.

On the day of Grandfather's funeral, Ken sat in the temple. He saw a framed picture of his grandfather in front of the urn. The sweet smell of burning incense filled the air.

Many relatives were at the temple. Ken knew most of them. But some had come from far away, and he had never met them before.

They prayed over the urn. They shook hands with Ken's crying father, and tried to comfort him.

Some relatives patted Ken on the back. They tried to cheer him up.

Ken just stared straight ahead.

Grandfather had moved into Ken's house for the last year of his life. He took over Ken's room.

Ken and his family took care of Grandfather for the entire year. At first, Grandfather had been his usual, cheerful self. But as he grew sicker, Grandfather changed. He looked sad. He slept more. He grew unable to talk, and would just stare out of the window into the sky.

Then, one warm summer night, he died.

AT THE TEMPLE, Ken found it hard to look at his grandfather's picture. Then, right before the funeral started, Ken's father touched Ken's shoulder. He nodded at the urn. Ken understood.

He knelt by the urn. Ken stared at the picture of his grandfather. He closed his eyes and said a prayer. Then he imagined himself talking to his grandfather. But it was no good. There was no answer.

The funeral seemed to last forever. Throughout it, four Buddhist monks with shaved heads sat in a row, chanting in low, serious voices.

Afterward, everyone came to Ken's house. His mother had prepared a big meal. The relatives sat around, telling stories about Grandfather. They laughed and had a good time.

Ken grew angry. How dare they laugh right after the funeral? After all, they weren't around when Grandfather was sick. They didn't visit him every single day as he approached death.

Ken's thoughts were interrupted. An uncle that Ken had never met before was telling a story. It was about a time Ken's grandfather had played in a baseball league many, many years before.

Ken knew that story! His grandfather had once told it to him. He and Ken had gone to a ball game at Dodger Stadium. As they sat in the bleachers, Ken's grandfather told Ken stories about his baseball-playing days. Right in the middle of one of the stories, Ken's grandfather caught a foul ball. He gave it to Ken.

"Grandfather was a great ball player," Ken said. Everyone looked at him. Ken told them about the game they saw at Dodger Stadium, and the foul ball Grandfather had caught. He went on to describe how he and Grandfather later played catch with that ball. Ken told how Grandfather had taught him to throw a curve ball.

Ken's story reminded a cousin of the time Grandfather taught him to ride a bicycle.

As Ken listened, he felt a gentle hand on his shoulder. He looked up and saw his father. Ken smiled at him. For the first time in many days, Ken's father smiled, too.

They knew that Grandfather's memory would be with them always.

ঽ঴

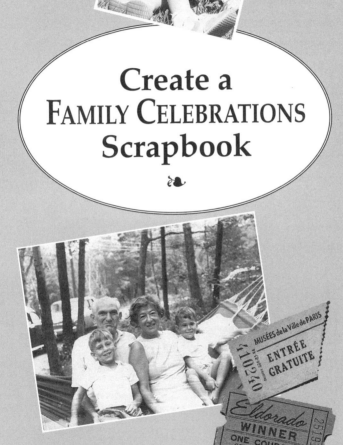

Create a
FAMILY CELEBRATIONS
Scrapbook

❧

H AVE YOU EVER taken part in a family celebration? Then you know how much fun they can be. You also know how important it is to save the memories of those special times. Make a "Family Celebrations" scrapbook. Here's how:

● Gather Pictures. Find photographs taken at family celebrations. Look for group photos that show everyone who was there. Also look for "action" shots that show people having a good time. (Make sure you have permission to use the pictures.)

● Keep Souvenirs. Not all family celebrations are important milestones. If you all go to a ball game and have a great time, that's a family celebration. If you go out for hamburgers, that could be a family celebration, too. Save the ticket stubs from the ball game.

Or bring home a paper place mat from the restaurant and have everyone sign it. These keepsakes are called souvenirs. Save them for your scrapbook.

● Collect Newspaper Articles. Notices for many milestones—such as weddings or christenings—will appear in newspapers. Cut them out and save them.

You can also find newspaper headlines for anniversaries. On what day were your parents married? You can probably find a copy of the newspaper from that day in your town's library. The newspaper shows what else was happening in the world that day. Make a photocopy of the front page. You can put it in your scrapbook with the page on their wedding anniversary.

• Talk to People Who Were There. Ask them questions about the celebrations. Make your questions straightforward. Ask things like, "What will you always remember about the celebration?" Talk to adults and children in order to get different points of view. Carefully write down their answers.

• Put It All Together. Get pieces of heavy construction paper. Carefully tape photos, souvenirs, or newspaper clippings onto the piece of construction paper. Neatly write down funny and interesting quotes from people who were there. Be sure to record the date of the celebration at the top of each sheet.

When you're done, put the scrapbook together. Carefully punch holes in the upper-left-hand corner of each page of your scrapbook. Include a front and back cover. Thread a colorful ribbon through the holes, and tie the pages together.

Now you have a Family Celebrations scrapbook. Add new pages to it as you and your family enjoy new special times.

Glossary

&

aunt
A sister of your mother or father.

baptism
A Christian ceremony welcoming a person
into the faith. The priest asks if the baby
accepts the Christian faith. The godparents
answer "yes" for the baby. Then the baby is
sprinkled with holy water. The godparents
promise to help raise the baby in the faith.
Some Protestant churches baptize only
adults.

bar mitzvah
bat mitzvah
These are words in Hebrew, a language used
by Jewish people. The words mean "son of
the commandment" and "daughter of the

commandment." They stand for ceremonies that celebrate a person's "coming of age" when he or she is thirteen years old.

bris
A Jewish ceremony for baby boys. At a bris, a family friend or relative holds the baby. A person called a mohel circumcises the baby. Wine is placed on the baby's lips, and many prayers are said for the baby.

brother-in-law
Your spouse's brother.

cousin
A child of your aunt or uncle.

father-in-law
Your spouse's father.

funeral
A ceremony held to honor a dead person. It usually is held right before the person's body is buried or cremated.

in-laws
Your spouse's family.

marriage
A ceremony where two people promise to spend the rest of their lives together. All religions have a marriage ceremony. Some people are married without a religious ceremony.

mother-in-law
Your spouse's mother.

namakaran
A Hindu ceremony for naming a baby. The entire family will gather at a party held in honor of the baby.

reunion
A party where people who have not seen each other for some time get together and visit. Many families hold family reunions every few years.

sister-in-law
Your spouse's sister.

spouse
The person you are married to.

synagogue
A Jewish temple.

tahara
An Islamic ceremony for baby boys. It is similar to a Jewish bris.

Torah
The Jewish holy book.

uncle
A brother of your mother or father.

ABOUT THE AUTHOR

Diane Patrick lives in the Bronx, New York. She has written biographies of Martin Luther King, Jr. and Coretta Scott King. She also writes for the children's newspaper *Harambee*.

ABOUT THE ILLUSTRATOR

Michael Bryant lives in Newark, New Jersey. He has drawn pictures for many books. Every day is a "family celebration" for Michael, his wife Gina, and their daughters Kristen and Allison.